A Christmas Fantasy

7 Late Intermediate to Early Advanced
Carol Arrangements for the Piano

DENNIS ALEXANDER

Foreword

This collection of arrangements is sure to be enjoyed by both teachers and their intermediate to advanced piano students. It contains a variety of performance styles which will appeal to the tastes of every student. Energetic, tender, lyrical, jazzy, robust—all of these moods permeate the music of this collection of Christmas favorites!

I trust that both teachers and students will enjoy sharing them with friends and family this Christmas season and for many years to come. Merry Christmas and best wishes for peace and happiness!

Dennis Alexander

Contents

To my parents, Bea and Norman, with love and appreciation.

Silent Night

Franz Grüber
Arr. by Dennis Alexander

What Child Is This?

Old English Melody
Arr. by Dennis Alexander

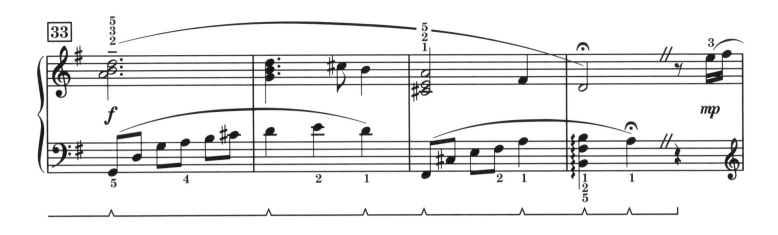

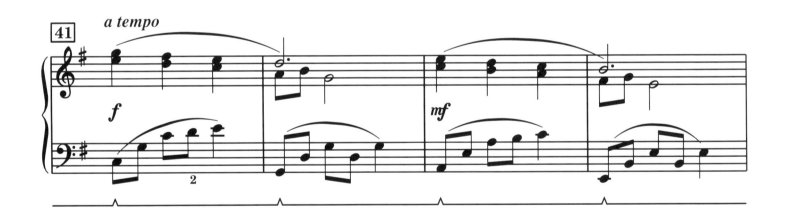

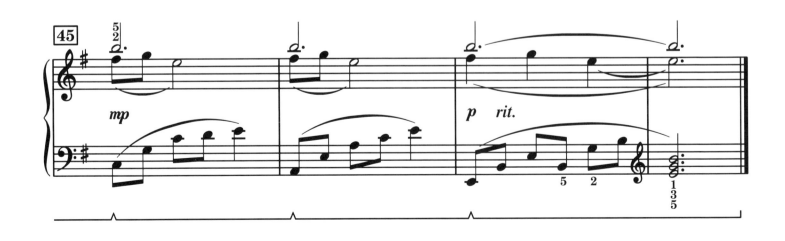

He Is Born, the Divine Christ Child

18th Century French Carol
Arr. by Dennis Alexander

8

Hark! the Herald Angels Sing

Felix Mendelssohn
Arr. by Dennis Alexander

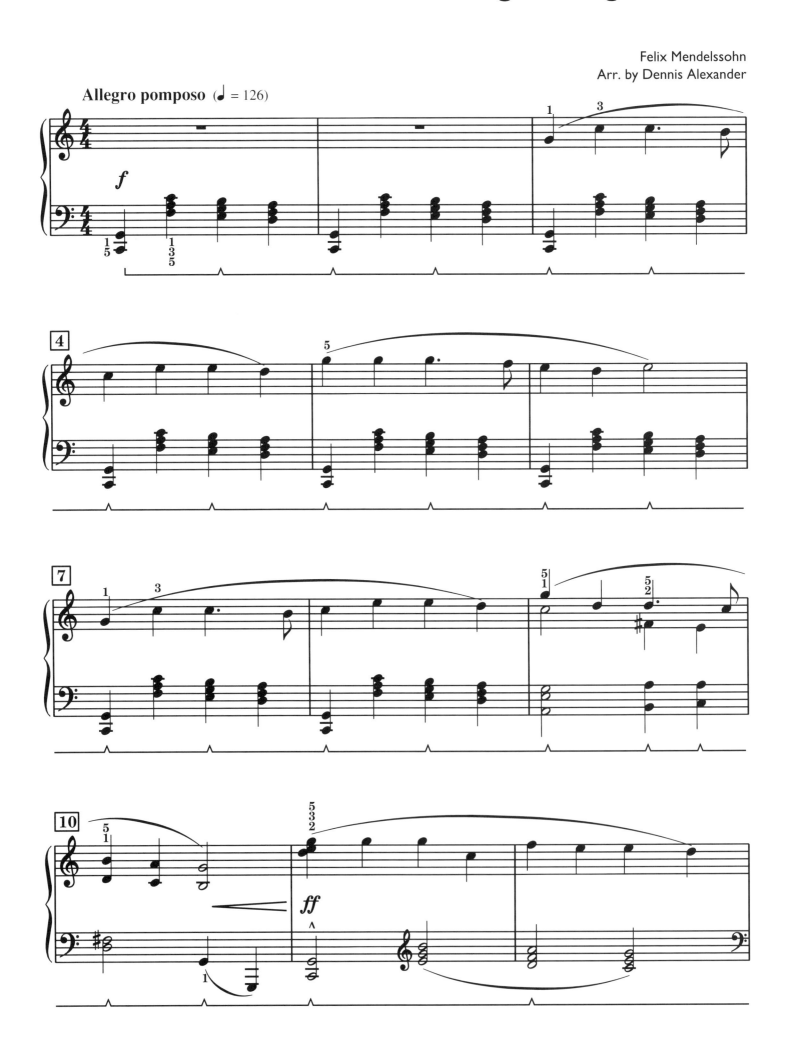

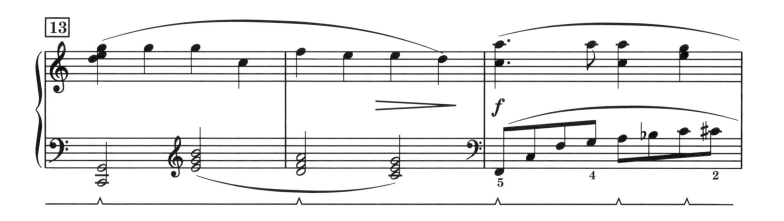

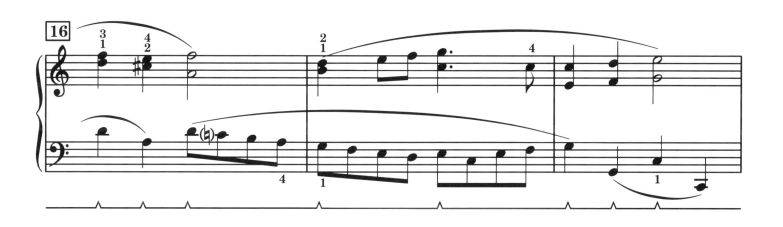

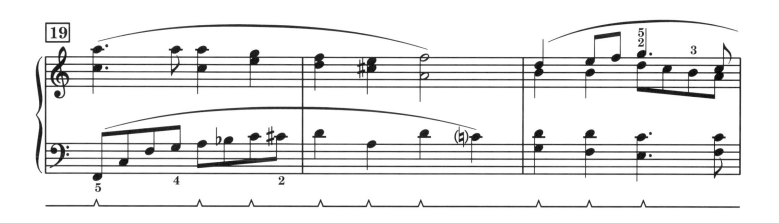

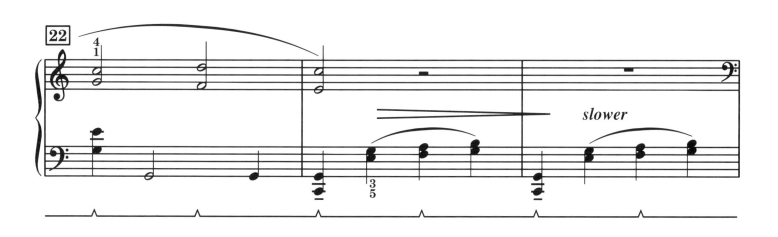

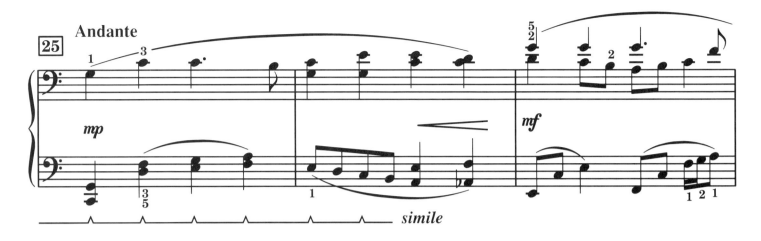

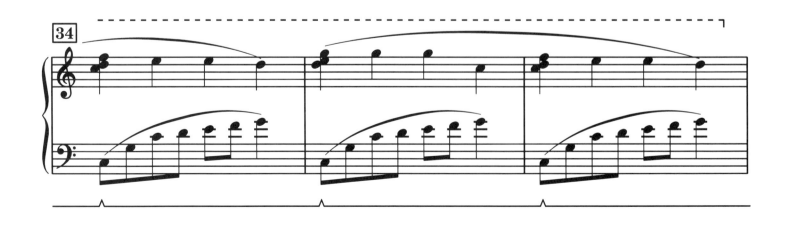

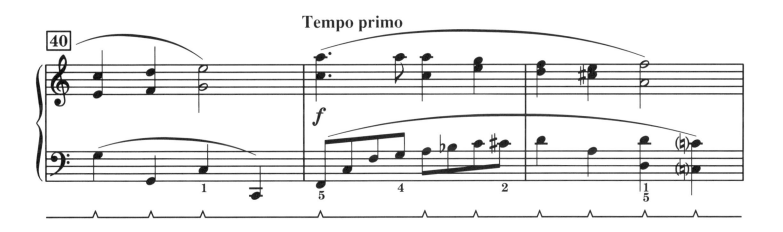

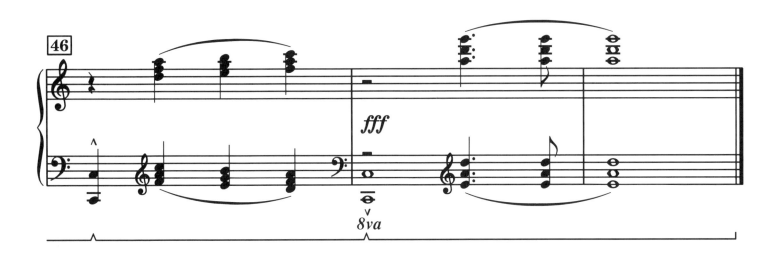

God Rest Ye Merry, Gentlemen

Traditional
Arr. by Dennis Alexander

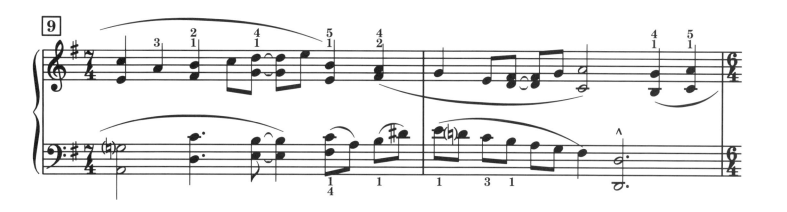

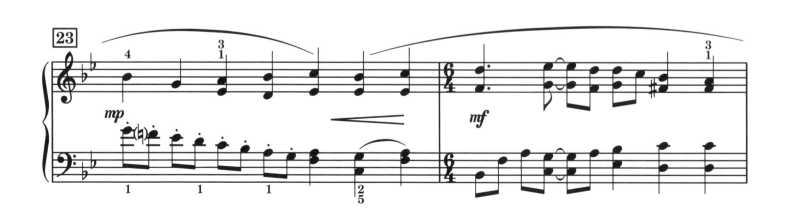

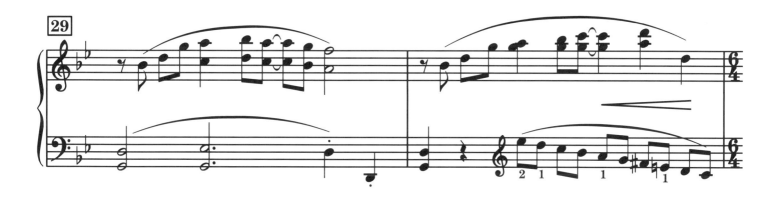

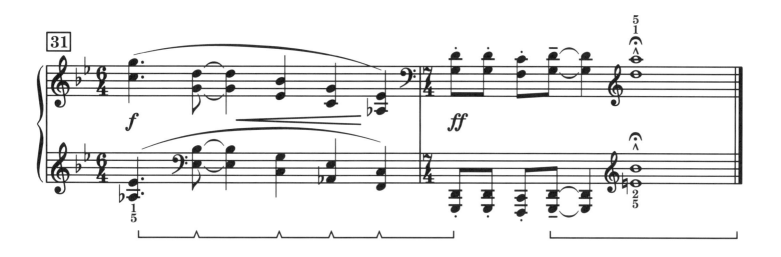

Still, Still, Still

Austrian
Arr. by Dennis Alexander

It Came Upon the Midnight Clear

Richard S. Willis
Arr. by Dennis Alexander

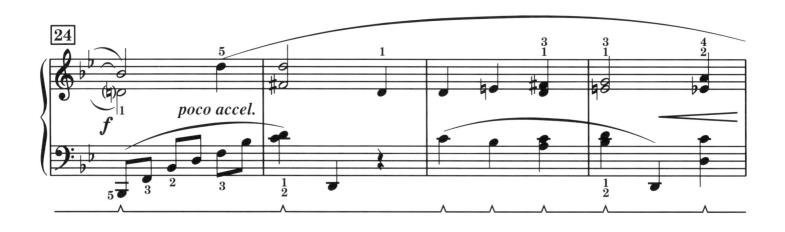

Dennis Alexander

Since his affiliation with Alfred Publishing Company in 1986 as a composer and clinician, Dennis Alexander has earned an international reputation as one of the foremost composers of educational piano music for beginning and intermediate students. Currently a professor of piano at the University of Montana, Missoula, he teaches both piano performance and piano pedagogy, and coordinates the piano division. In 1987 he made his New York debut at Carnegie Recital Hall with violinist Walter Olivares and continues to be active as a soloist, accompanist and chamber musician.

Mr. Alexander is a past president of the Montana Music Teachers Association and has been a featured speaker at national conventions of the Music Teachers National Association (MTNA). In addition to writing all the duet books for Alfred's Basic Piano Library, he has recorded much of this successful method. His extensive output includes solo and duet repertoire in collections and sheet music for beginning through early advanced students.